Beautiful North AMERICA

Majestic Landscapes from Sea to Shining Sea

By Minju Pak

Photography by Quang-Tuan Luong

This a Parragon Publishing Book

Conceived and produced by

Glitterati Incorporated/www.GlitteratiIncorporated.com

First published in 2006 by

Parragon Publishing

Queen Street House

4 Queen Street

Bath BA1 1HE, UK

Design by Sarah Morgan Karp

ISBN: 978-1-4054-8010-9

Beautiful North
AMERICA

Majestic Landscapes from Sea to Shining Sea

By Minju Pak

Photography by Quang-Tuan Luong

Dedication

To mom, dad, Joe, and Ian
and, especially, for halmoni

Acknowledgments

Thanks to Marta, for the opportunities
Sarah, for your talent
QT, for your eye, which made this book what it is

Contents

Chapter 1

New England

Far left, Old State House and modern buildings in downtown. Boston, Massachussetts, USA. Left, Quechee Gorge in fall. Vermont, New England, USA.

It's been called "heaven and earth"; where the "air is sweet and clear, the heavens serene"; and no place "better for a man's habitation." Better known today as the birthplace of America, New England — comprised of Connecticut, Maine, Massachusetts, New Hampshire, Rhode Island, and Vermont — caught the attention of early settlers, who recognized the splendor that was to become the New World.

It's easy to imagine the lure of this northeastern corner of the country — even now, after centuries of modernization. From its serrated coastline to its mountain peaks, from its cultural institutions to its urban centers, New England provides some of the most beautiful scenery in the world. The region's highest peak resides on New Hampshire's Mount Washington (6,288 ft. above sea level), within the state's White Mountain National Forest, where views from the summit span four states, Quebec, and the Atlantic Ocean. The area is sprinkled with lakes, rivers, swamps, and sandy beaches. At 410 miles long, the Connecticut River is the area's longest, navigating through four states and responsible for 70% of Long Island Sound's freshwater, while Lake Champlain, which lies between Vermont and New York, is its largest lake. Out of the six states, Vermont is the only one without a coastline — and, coincidentally, is also the least populated. New England's beaches provide some of the most eminent stretches of land in the country, most notably Massachusetts' Cape Cod, Martha's Vineyard and Nantucket. Although these have secured a firm slot in this culture's vernacular as popular destinations, the region is also known for its less-glitzy neighbors: Maine's coastline, for its small, outlying islands, fresh lobster and rural beauty; Newport, Rhode Island, for its outdoor festivals and centuries-old historical architecture; and Hampton Beach in New Hampshire.

Frenchman Bay from Cadillac mountain,
Acadia National Park, Maine, USA.

The frozen Charles River seen from the Prudential Tower. Boston, Massachussetts, USA.

New England

Sleepy Hollow Farm near Woodstock. Vermont, New England, USA.

Above, A mix of colorful trees. Acadia National Park, Maine, USA.
Above right, White birches and red maples. Acadia National Park, Maine, USA.

Boston is the area's most populous city, while Providence, Rhode Island, and Waterbury, Connecticut, are also in the top 10 in terms of population. Come September, the area is rife with students, as it houses eight of the country's top 50 universities, including its most well-known Ivy Leagues: Harvard and Yale.

Though the western half of the country takes most of the credit for America's national parks, New England has its fair share of unadulterated parkland. Stretching from Chatham and Provincetown, Cape Cod in Massachusetts, this seaside park stretches 40 miles, with over 40 acres of beaches, ponds, marshes, and dunes. The Appalachian National Scenic Trail is a true state connector, as it passed through almost every state in New England, excluding Maine and Rhode Island, as well as through others, including Maryland, West Virginia, and down through Tennessee. Maine's Acadia National Park is one of the region's most spectacular, with over 47,000 acres of woodlands, lakes, mountains and beaches. It's been said that Acadia's own Cadillac Mountains, which reach 1,530 feet, is the point where the sunrise touches first before any place in this country.

But, it's all about the fall.

Through all of its geographical variety, though, New England is synonymous with autumn. It's the region's busiest tourism season, when out-of-towners come to witness the spectacular flashes of bold colors — oranges, reds, yellows, greens, purples and everything in between — the transformation of nature that compares to nowhere else in the world. But the main fall foliage season lasts for about a month — between the end of September and end of October. Literary giants were inspired by this region's climate. By the majesty it provides, as Ralph Waldo Emerson calls when "the world reaches its perfection"; and by its unpredictability, as Mark Twain wrote, "In the spring I have counted one hundred and thirty-six different kinds of weather inside of four-and-twenty hours."

Truck loaded with pumpkins. New Hampshire, New England, USA.

Covered bridge, Bath. New Hampshire, New England, USA

Above, Bass Harbor lighthouse, sunset. Acadia National Park, Maine, USA. Right,
Old man of the mountain, Franconia Notch. New Hampshire, New England, USA.

Autumn Reflexions, Green Mountains. Vermont, New England, USA.

New England

Village of East Corinth surrounded by fall colors, early morning. Vermont, New England, USA.

Above, Water cascade over smooth rock, Franconia Notch. New Hampshire, New England, USA.
Right, Moss Glen Falls, Green Mountains. Vermont, New England, USA.

　　　　　　　New England

Chapter 2

The Mid Atlantic

Left, Chrysler building, seen from the Empire State building at dusk. New York City, USA. Right, Spining leaves and cascade. Shenandoah National Park, Virginia, USA.

Left, Chrysler building, seen from the Empire State building at dusk. New York City, USA. Right, Spining leaves and cascade. Shenandoah National Park, Virginia, USA.

Whether you prefer to call it the Northeast Corridor, the Baltimore-Washington Metropolitan area or the Mid-Atlantic states, some of the most populated — and popular — cities in North America inhabit this area between New England and the South. Philadelphia, Baltimore, Washington DC, and the country's largest city, New York City, are clustered here. With access to waterways, historically, the region provided heavy industry and a destination for America's "melting pot." Today, its cities are still some of the most ethnically diverse in the country.

The landmarks in the region are some of the most famous in the world, and sound off as a laundry list of this country's history: New York City's Statue of Liberty, Ellis Island, the Empire State Building; Philadelphia's Independence Hall, the Liberty Bell; and the National Mall in the nation's capital, which features numerous memorials to leaders and events. Though this region is better known for its urban centerpieces, its outlying areas have an attraction all their own — both beautiful and original to its environment. While Maryland is the country's most narrow state, Delaware is its second smallest. The Delaware River, which borders on a few of the Mid-Atlantics — creating a partial boundary between Pennsylvania and New York, a complete boundary between New Jersey and Pennsylvania and Delaware and New Jersey — is 410 miles long, and is well-known for President George Washington's "Delaware crossing," the body of water in which the country's first president traversed during the American Revolution. Pennsylvania's south-central region is home to more than 15 sects of the Pennsylvania Dutch, including the Mennonites and Amish and, for this reason, has become a popular tourist destination.

Ridges in haze seen from Clingmans Dome. Great
Smoky Mountains National Park, Tennessee, USA.

Skyline Drive in autumn. Shenandoah National Park, Virginia, USA.

The Mid Atlantic

Mabry Mill, Blue Ridge Parkway. Virginia, USA

Above, Tree with spring foliage standing against the sky. Shenandoah National Park, Virginia, USA. Left, Redbud trees in bloom. Virginia, USA. Right, Arching dogwood in bloom, Middle Prong of the Little River. Great Smoky Mountains National Park, Tennessee, USA.

The Mid Atlantic

Black Rock, sunset. Shenandoah National Park, Virginia, USA.

The Mid Atlantic

East Building of the National Gallery, designed by Pei. Washington DC, USA.

Above left, The Wall, Vietnam Veterans Memorial. Washington DC, USA. Above right, The National Mall and Washington monument seen from the Capitol, sunset. Washington DC, USA.

This region also boasts the country's only "America in Miniature," as Maryland has been deemed. Though it's the narrowest state, it's rich in topography. From lush sea grass growing in marshland to pine groves to sandy, hilly dunes, Maryland also has an inordinate variety of flora, from palm trees to maples to reeds. Virginia provides the country with its Shenandoah National Park, which has six waterfalls and 500 miles of trails, 100 of which are part of the Appalachian Trail. The park is best known for its Skyline Drive, a 105-mile road that runs along the Blue Ridge Mountains — one of the most famous mountain range in the country. The Blue Ridge runs from the Carolinas to New York State, with over 400 miles linking Shenandoah to the Great Smoky Mountains.

Though these Mid-Atlantic states gradate from the eastern to southern portions of this country, the centerpiece is, arguably, the island that runs only 13 miles long and 2.3 miles across. Manhattan has many nicknames — the Big Apple, the "city that never sleeps," to name only a couple — and is one of the most famous cities in the world, with over one million people residing on the island. A giant in every imaginable industry, the city has inspired crooners to "start spreading the news" and "take a walk on the wild side."

Above left, Statue of Liberty against sky. New York City, USA. Right, Wall Street stock exchange. New York City, USA.
Above. Midtown and Upper Manhattan, seen from the World Trade Center. New York City, USA.

Chapter 3

The Southeast

The Southeast may not have the same recognizable ring that regions such as the Midwest or New England does, but it is one of the most significant areas in the country. Included in the mix are states such as Georgia, North Carolina, South Carolina, and Florida — the latter of which has become one of the most dominant states in culture and politics in this country.

Between the Gulf of Mexico, the Atlantic Ocean, and the Straits of Florida, the state of Florida is bordered by Georgia and Alabama. Britton Hill is the highest point in the state, but it is still the lowest of any high point in the country. Known for destinations such as Disneyworld and Miami Beach, Florida has much more to offer in terms of its landscape. The plethora of national parks themselves demonstrate the array of scenery that the state offers.

Everglades National Park, which spans over 2,000 miles, boasts landmarks such as the Pahayokee Overlook, an elevated area where visitors can look down onto the expanse of the park to the north; the Royal Palm, which showcases the wooded pine area; and the Mahogany Hammock, a trail that runs through a large cypress swamp. The Everglades is the only place, besides Louisiana, where crocodiles can be found. One of the best-known destinations in Florida is the Florida Keys, which is a sequence of about 1,700 islands. The islands, which reside along the Florida Straits, divide the Atlantic Ocean from the Gulf of Mexico.

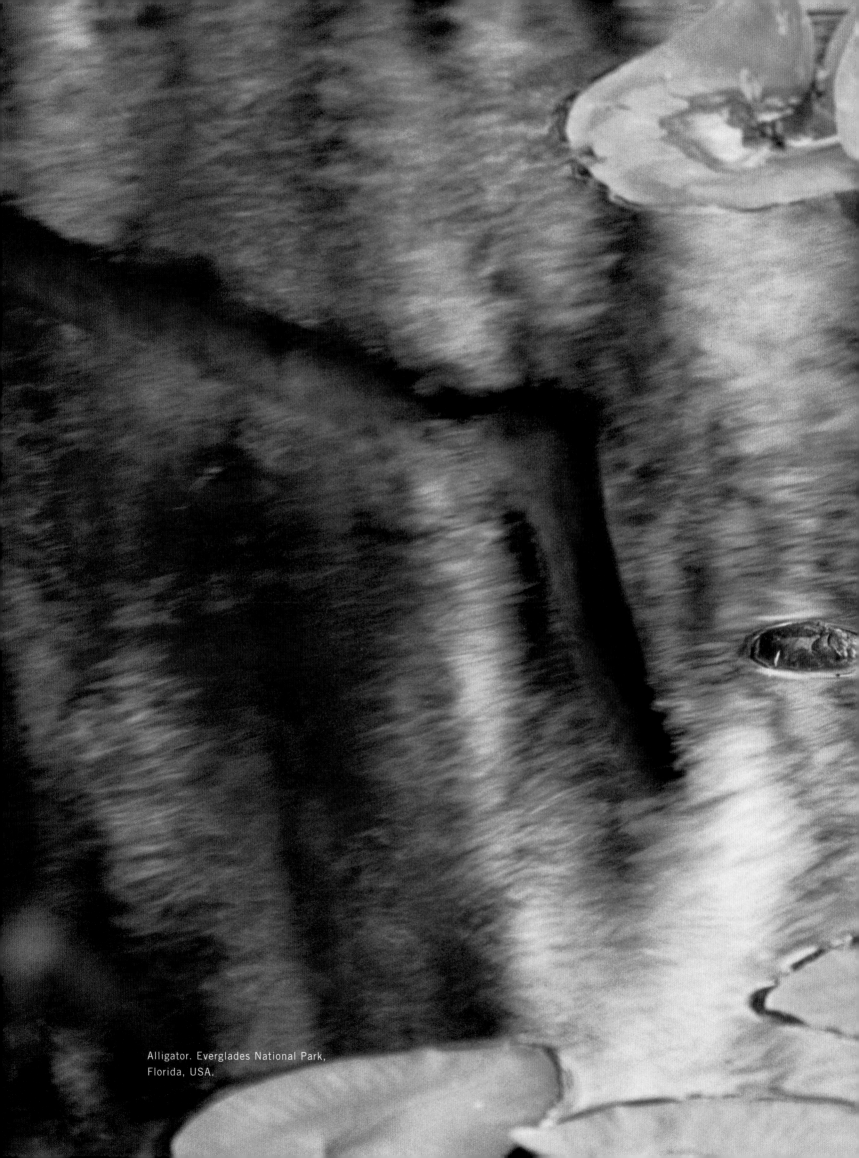

Alligator. Everglades National Park,
Florida, USA.

Above, Mangroves on Elliott Key. Biscayne National Park, Florida, USA. Right, Saltwarts plants and tree on the outer coast, morning, Elliott Key. Biscayne National Park, Florida, USA.

Above left, School of baitfish fleeing a predator. Biscayne National Park, Florida, USA. Above right, Yellow snappers and soft coral. Biscayne National Park, Florida, USA.

Beach and Fort Jefferson. Dry Tortugas National Park, Florida, USA.

Above, Seawall at dusk during a storm. Dry Tortugas National Park, Florida, USA. Left, Fort Jefferson seawall and moat, framed by a crumpling cannon window, late afternoon. Dry Tortugas National Park, Florida, USA.

Though lesser known, South Carolina's Congaree National Park contains over 22,000 acres, making it one of this country's smallest national parks. The trees that occupy this park are some of the tallest in the East, and the park contains the largest expanse of hardwood forest. Georgia's High Falls State Park used to be an industrial town, with its own shoe shop, blacksmith, and cotton gin. Most frequented in the park are its lush waterfalls, along with its 650-acre lake, which is open to fishing.

When it comes to bodies of water, Florida's beaches are world-renowned. Miami Beach has become a hotspot among celebrities and the rich and famous, but it is because the state has preserved its wildlife that its coastlines have been able to remain so beautiful. The state's Biscayne National Park spans over 207 miles, including one of the most popular scuba diving areas in the United States. With 95 percent of the park covered in water, the park is mainly for these divers who come to experience one of the best spots in the Atlantic.

Slash pines at sunrise, near Mahogany Hammock.
Everglades National Park, Florida, USA.

Above, Pines and palmetto. Corkscrew Swamp, Florida, USA. Center, Cypress trunk detail. Congaree National Park, South Carolina, USA. Far right, Cypress and swamp in summer. Congaree National Park, South Carolina, USA.

Sunset on mangroves. The Keys, Florida, USA.

Ahinga. Everglades National Park, Florida, USA.

Above, Facade of Hemingway's house. Key West, Florida, USA. Below, Spanish moss, Okefenokee Swamp. Georgia, USA. Left, Old and new Seven-mile bridges. The Keys, Florida, USA.

Above left, Okefenokee Swamp at sunset. Georgia, USA. Above right, Aligator in the back of a water lettuce pond.
Corkscrew Swamp, Florida, USA

Sailboats viewed against the sun disk at sunset. Key West, Florida, USA.

Above, Grasses at sunset, Hilton Head. South Carolina, USA. Left,
Tiny crabs, Hilton Head. South Carolina, USA.

Chapter 4

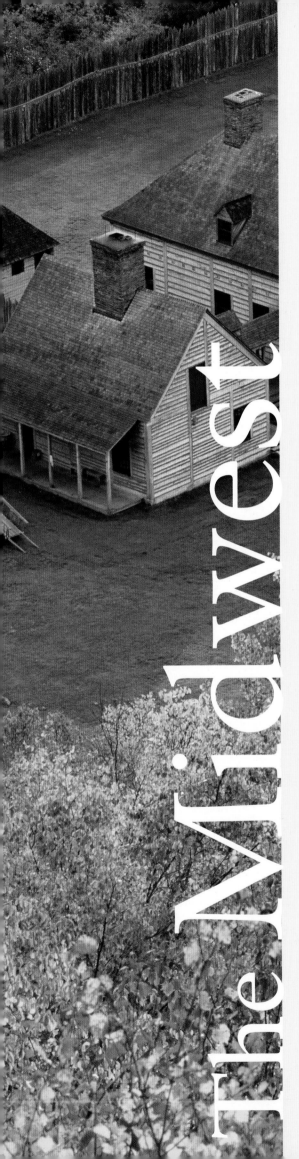

The Midwest

Bordered by the Great Lakes and the Ohio and Mississippi River Valleys, the Midwest may not, geographically, be the center of this country but that doesn't seem to matter. Some have nicknamed it "middle America" but it's most fondly known as the "heartland." Like any region in this country, the terms given to them connote more of a state of being, a personality, rather than a location.

Midwesterners are known to be down-to-earth, grounded, open yet frank. As they can claim rivers and lakes as their main bodies of waters, the Mississippi River, specifically, has acted as the major pathway for settlers to travel through to arrive to the region throughout its history. Priding itself on core values, such as modesty, simplicity, and hard work, the region has contributed significantly to the culture: The Republican Party was formed in the 1850s in the Midwest; native Missourian, Samuel Clemens, a.k.a. Mark Twain, was inspired by the area's Mississippi River, writing two books centering around it (*Life on the Mississippi* and *Adventures of Huckleberry Finn*); it spawned the Progressive Movement, consisting mainly of the area's farmers and merchants, to shine a spotlight on the dangers of corruption in the government.

Today, the nation's third largest city, Chicago, Illinois, is in the Midwest, accommodating one of the tallest buildings in the world: the famous Sears Tower. But it also claims major cities such as Cleveland and Columbus, both in Ohio; Detroit, Michigan; Madison, Wisconsin; and Minneapolis, Minnesota. While geographically, the region is generally flat, what its forefathers were enticed by in the beginning — its rich farmlands — still exist today. The Midwest is split mostly by urban and agricultural areas — the latter of which consist mostly of corn and soy, wheat and range lands.

Sable falls in autumn, Pictured Rocks National
Lakeshore. Upper Michigan Peninsula, USA

The Mid West

The region's lesser-known contributions are what make this area the most spectacular, which are its various mountain ranges and parks, spanning hundreds of miles with personalities all their own. Michigan's Porcupine Mountains Wilderness State Park houses the Porcupine Mountains, or Porkies, as they are called. The mountain range extends across the northwestern Upper Peninsula of the state, near Lake Superior.

Ohio's only national park, the Cuyahoga Valley National Park, crosses over 51 miles along the state's Cuyahoga River, between Akron and Cleveland. For the state of Minnesota, it took nearly 80 years for the country to declare land for a national park. Land for a national park in the state of Minnesota was first proposed to the president of the United States in 1891. Eighty years later, President Richard Nixon would sign into law delineating national park land in Minnesota, officially naming it Voyageurs National Park. The heart of the Amnicon Falls State Park in Wisconsin is its Amnicon River, which is 30 miles long and crosses over eight counties. Wisconsin's varied wilderness also offers the Apostle Islands National Lakeshore, with what some consider as one of the finest groups of historic lighthouses in the country. With over 21 islands, holding names such as Bear Island, Hermit Island, Cat Island, Otter Island and Raspberry Island, the land offers over 154 miles of shoreline.

When it comes to shoreline, though, one of the greatest attractions of the Midwest are, without a doubt, the Great Lakes, and Lake Michigan is its centerpiece. The only lake in the bunch that is situated entirely within the United States, while the others are shared with Canada, Lake Michigan is one of a kind on many fronts: It's the largest freshwater lake in the U.S.; the largest lake entirely in one country; and the fifth largest lake in the world. At 307 miles long and 118 miles wide, its beaches are known for its high quartz content, revealed by the squeaking sounds made when one walks across the sand. In Northern Michigan, the beaches along the lake are the only places in the world where visitors can come upon Petoskey stones, the state stone of Michigan.

Above left, Islands of the Isle Royale archipelago. Isle Royale National Park, Michigan, USA. Below left, Eroded granite on Mount Franklin. Isle Royale National Park, Michigan, USA.

Right, Moose antlers, Windego. Isle Royale National Park, Michigan, USA. Center, Mist on Kendall lake. Cuyahoga Valley National Park, Ohio, USA. Left, Sandstone depression at The Ledges. Cuyahoga Valley National Park, Ohio, USA.

Above, Coast on Rock Harbor trail. Isle Royale National Park, Michigan, USA. Left, Lake with red maple in fall colors, Hiawatha National Forest. Upper Michigan Peninsula, USA.

Right, Miners castle, late afternoon, Pictured Rocks National Lakeshore. Upper Michigan Peninsula, USA. Above, River and trees in autumn colors, Porcupine Mountains State Park. Upper Michigan Peninsula, USA.

The Mid West

Right, River. Chicago, Illinois, USA. Center, Sears tower framed by other skyscrappers. Chicago, Illinois, USA. Above, Skyline of the city above Lake Michigan, morning. Chicago, Illinois, USA.

Wharf building in Lake Superior at dusk, Apostle Islands National Lakeshore. Wisconsin, USA

The Mid West

Sunset over Lake Superior, Apostle Islands National Lakeshore. Wisconsin, USA.

Birch tree trunks. Voyageurs National Park, Minnesota, USA.

The Mid West

Pond surrounded by trees in fall colors. Wisconsin, USA.

Left, Rainy lake. Voyageurs National Park, Minnesota, USA. Above, Beaver pond. Voyageurs National Park, Minnesota, USA.

Amnicon Falls State Park. Wisconsin, USA

The Mid West

Loons, early morning on Chippewa harbor. Isle Royale National Park, Michigan, USA.

Lake Superior seen through trees at sunset, Pictured Rocks National Lakeshore. Upper Michigan Peninsula, USA.
Right, Cascades near Bridalveil falls. Cuyahoga Valley National Park, Ohio, USA.

The Mid West

Chapter 5

The Great Plains

Left, Windmill and tractor under a threatening stormy sky. North Dakota, USA. Far left, Cannon balls. Theodore Roosevelt National Park, North Dakota, USA.

Thoughts of a prairie land rarely evoke images of erosion formations, paleontology discoveries, and buttes whose colors range from warms reds to midnight blues, depending on the time of year. Though the Great Plains are known for its seemingly limitless stretch of prairie, parks such as South Dakota's Badlands National Park merge the flat prairie landscape with preserved spires that jut out of the earth. Nebraska's Scotts Bluff National Monument is another natural phenomenon that preserves land formations that protrude above the Plains below.

East of the Rocky Mountains, the Great Plains, in its earliest days, became land for open range ranching, making it legal for anyone to run cattle. Throughout the generations, though, the region has seen the change from utilization for cattle ranching to valuable crop-growing. Level prairie land consume a portion of this region, but one section of the land can greatly differ from the next, which has made the Great Plains one of the most original areas in the country. From the High Plains, which extend south from the northern border of Nebraska through Texas, to the Black Hills and their dark forests, which can be seen from any direction, the Plains defy all notions of what inland territory looks like.

Spreading over 242,000 acres, Badlands National Park is the perfect example of what this region brings to the landscape of America. A blend of grassy prairie below juxtaposes with deep cuts into the land, where formations protrude into the sky. The history of the park goes back to traditional Native American knowledge of the area, when large fossilized bones, seashells, and turtle shells were found. With the evidence on hand, the Native Americans correctly realized that the area had once been underwater, housing bones from animals that do not exist today.

Sheep Mountain table. Badlands National Park, South Dakota, USA.

The Great Plains

Erosion formations, Cedar Pass, dawn. Badlands National Park, South Dakota, USA.

Moon and erosion formations, Cedar Pass, dawn.
Badlands National Park, South Dakota, USA.

Above left, Caprock chimneys, Caprock coulee trail, North Unit. Theodore Roosevelt National Park, North Dakota, USA. Above right, View from Pinacles overlook, sunrise. Badlands National Park, South Dakota, USA. Right, Pedestal petrified log and badlands, late afternoon. Theodore Roosevelt National Park, North Dakota, USA.

Above, Hay rolls. Nebraska, USA. Right, Yellow field with rolls of hay.
North Dakota, USA.

Above right, Old wagons and bluff. Scotts Bluff National Monument. Nebraska, USA. Above left, Prairie Dog town, South Unit. Theodore Roosevelt National Park, North Dakota, USA. Left, Roosevelt's Maltese Cross Cabin, afternoon. Theodore Roosevelt National Park, North Dakota, USA.

The same state commemorates American history, with one of the most popular tourist attractions in the world: Mount Rushmore. Near Keystone, South Dakota, the Memorial was erected to represent the first 150 years of U.S. history., with 60-foot sculptures of presidents George Washington, Thomas Jefferson, Abraham Lincoln, and Thomas Jefferson carved into the side of a mountain. With over two million visitors every year, the site covers over one thousand acres and is over five thousand feet above sea level.

For a more focused look at one of this country's most revered presidents, the Theodore Roosevelt National Park was established in 1978 in North Dakota. The former president owned and worked on a ranch preserved in the park. Roosevelt had retreated to the ranch after the death of his mother and wife and recorded his experiences on the land in articles for newspapers and magazines.

For a slice of regional history, though, Scotts Bluff National Monument in western Nebraska is where the vast prairie that the region is known for can be appreciated in all of its glory. Though the site has multiple bluffs, the area includes several landmarks, including one on the Oregon Trail and Mormon Trail. Its namesake, Scotts Bluff, rises over 830 feet above the plains' highest point, and the monument is comprised of five rock formations: Crown Rock, Dome Rock, Eagle Rock, Saddle Rock, and Sentinel Rock.

Above, Storm cloud over prairie. South Dakota, USA. Right, Scotts Bluff at sunrise. Scotts Bluff National Monument. Nebraska, USA.

The Great Plains

Left, Tall grass and hills at Bison Flats, sunrise. Wind Cave National Park, South Dakota, USA. Above, Flowers, trees on skyline, morning. Wind Cave National Park, South Dakota, USA.

Alley of the Flags, with flags from each of the 50 US states, Mt Rushmore National Memorial. South Dakota, USA.
George Washington profile, Mount Rushmore National Memorial. South Dakota, USA.

The Great Plains

Chapter 6

The Mountain States

Derived from the Spanish word montaña, meaning "mountain," Montana is a state indicative of this region. Larger-than-life mountain ranges, open sky, deep-blue lakes, and rolling hills are found in almost every state in these Mountain States, but nature doesn't stop there.

Yellowstone National Park, the first and oldest national park in the world resides in the states of Wyoming, Montana, and Idaho — the Mountain States region. Covering over three thousand square miles, the majority of the park is in the northwest corner of Wyoming, while Montana claims three of the five entrances to Yellowstone. Named after the headwaters of the Yellowstone River, the park is best known for its spewing geysers and hot springs, both of which set this national park apart from others in the country. The park is truly a wonder of nature, sharing its resources from both sides of the Continental Divide of North America. Running diagonally through the southwestern part of the park, the Divide is a ridgeline that splits the country between the Pacific and Atlantic Ocean water drainages. Thus, a third of the park is on the Pacific side, while the rest relies on the drainages from the Atlantic end. The park is closed in on all sides by spectacular mountain ranges of the Middle Rocky Mountains: the Gallatin Range to the northwest; the north presents the Beartooth Mountains; the east, the Absaroka Mountains; the Wind River Range is at the southeast corner; the Teton Mountains are to the South; and the Madison Range reside in the west end of the park.

An offshoot of the park, though entirely unique on its own accord, are the south end's Teton Mountains, which inspire a national park of its own. Named after the Grand Teton, the highest mountain within the national park, it is also the second highest in Wyoming. Reaching over 13,000 feet high, the mountain is part of the Rocky Mountains.

With all of the mountain ranges in the area and the name itself, "Mountain States," one of the region's major attractions is, ironically, the immensity of sky. Nicknamed "Big Sky Country," Montana is known for its endless blue sky. Though the mountains come up against it, the layout of the land, the geography of the region, and unknown other factors, contribute to something that other states don't seem to have. One would swear that the sky is substantial enough to envelop the earth in Montana.

The region may be able to claim the country's oldest national park, but it can also declare its youngest in the Great Sand Dunes National Park in Colorado. In a state known for its beautiful snow-covered winters, the park is thought of as a wonder of nature. Formed from sand deposits of the Rio Grande River, the dunes are thought to have been created by sand taken to the air by wind and, as the wind lost power, was set down. The formation continues to grow, as sand particles are still being flown over the area and dropped down. The dunes are over 12,000 years old, covering 19,000 acres and rising above 700 feet, making them the tallest sand dunes in North America.

Avalanche Creek. Glacier National Park, Montana, USA.

St Mary Lake, Wild Goose Island, sunrise. Glacier National Park, Montana, USA. Right, The Narrows in late afternoon. Black Canyon of the Gunnison National Park, Colorado, USA.

Above, The Gunisson river near the Narrows. Black Canyon of the Gunnison National Park, Colorado, USA. Below, Patch of sand in snow-covered dunes. Great Sand Dunes National Park, Colorado, USA.

Above, Icebergs in Upper Grinnel Lake, with glacier and Mt Gould in background. Glacier National Park, Montana, USA. Center, Distant view of dunes and Sangre de Christo mountains in late afternoon. Great Sand Dunes National Park, Colorado, USA.

Waterfall at hanging gardens, Logan pass. Glacier National Park, Montana, USA. Left, The Teton range above Jackson lake. Grand Teton National Park, Wyoming, USA.

Teton range and fall colors on meadows. Grand Teton National Park, Wyoming, USA. Left, Moulton Barn and Grand Tetons, morning. Grand Teton National Park, Wyoming, USA.

Above, Kiva in Balcony House. Mesa Verde National Park, Colorado, USA. Left, Cliff Palace, late afternoon. Mesa Verde National Park, Colorado, USA.

Alpine flowers and summer storma along Trail Ridge road. Rocky Mountain National Park, Colorado, USA. Left, Windy morning, Sprague Lake. Rocky Mountain National Park, Colorado, USA.

Sunrise on a pond in Horseshoe park. Rocky Mountain National Park, Colorado, USA.

Orange aspens and blue mountains. Colorado, USA.

Right, Waterfall near the Continental Divide. Colorado, USA. Above, Mesas, Monument Canyon view. Colorado, USA.

Pine on cinder cone and crescent moon, Craters
of the Moon National Monument, Idaho, USA.

Silver Gate at dawn. Wyoming, USA.

Devil's Tower, sunset, Devils Tower National Monument. Wyoming, USA.

Left, Minerva travertine terraces at Mammoth Hot Springs. Yellowstone National Park, Wyoming, USA. Right, Morning Glory Pool, midday. Yellowstone National Park, Wyoming, USA. Far right, Old Faithful Geyser, late afternoon. Yellowstone National Park, Wyoming, USA.

Chapter 7

Whether it's the region's history, cultural contribution, political influence, metropolitan areas, or its untouched natural beauty, the South is considered one of the most influential regions in this country. The South contains eight of the 25 largest urban centers in the U.S., yet geographically is one of the most diverse. From swampland to dry heat to the most spectacular lightning storms in the world, the region is extremely varied in regard to almost every aspect, making it difficult to categorize.

If it's not the cuisine, it's the music, literature, or art. It's one of the only regions in the country that has a distinct dialect. A Southerner can be heard and recognized by their accent or the language they use. Technically, Southern English can be divided into sub-dialects, ranging from the Appalachian and coastal area regions to the south midlands dialect. Houston, Dallas, and San Antonio, all in Texas, rank as three of the top-ten most-populated metropolitan areas in the region, with Atlanta, Georgia, also in the mix.

Though the area offers much culturally, with the influence of its cities, its mix of dry and humid climates provide breathtaking examples of natural scenery. In fact, some of the most beautiful parks are in the South, though most of them are considered lesser-known nature reserves.

Kentucky's Mammoth Cave National Park, located in the central portion of the state, offers the most extensive cave system known to the world today. Covering over 52,000 acres, the park curves around the Green River with more than 300 miles of passageway. The Guadalupe Mountains National Park contains the Guadalupe Peak, the highest point in Texas, reaching over 8,000 feet high. The park is best known for the

Yucca and El Capitan, early morning. Guadalupe Mountains National Park, Texas, USA. Center, Gypsum sand dunes and Guadalupe range at sunset. Guadalupe Mountains National Park, Texas, USA. Above right, Colorful prickly pear cactus in bloom and Chisos Mountains. Big Bend National Park, Texas, USA. Below right, Agaves on South Rim, evening. Big Bend National Park, Texas, USA.

Left, Limestone cliffs and trees in autumn color near Devil's Hall. Guadalupe Mountains National Park, Texas, USA. Above, Autumn colors and cliffs in McKittrick Canyon. Guadalupe Mountains National Park, Texas, USA.

Left, Trees and reflections in Echo River Spring. Mammoth Cave National Park, Kentucky, USA. Right, Stalagtites and stalagmites in the Frozen Niagara section. Mammoth Cave National Park, Kentucky, USA.

Pink and white Dogwoods in bloom, Bernheim arboretum. Kentucky, USA.

electric colors that strike out in the fall trees that reside in its McKittrick Canyon, which contrast against the earthy tones of the surrounding Chihuahuan desert. Most of all, though, the park is used for its incredible hiking trails, which take visitors through the varying landscape. The Guadalupe Peak Trail offers the "Top of Texas," where on a clear day hikers can reach the tip and look out onto the expanse of land; the Devil's Hall Trail takes people through the low canyons; and the Bowl cuts through pine forests.

Though it is the smallest national park in the country, the Hot Springs National Park in central Arkansas offers visitors a chance to dip into natural waters thought to aid in various ailments, including joint pain. The springs flow down from the Ouachita Mountain Range. While there are hiking trails, the park has also built bathhouses, where the natural spring water can be enjoyed indoors.

When one talks of rich history, profound contributions to the culture, and the hospitality of Southern people, the first city that comes to mind is New Orleans, Louisiana. Considered the birthplace of jazz, the city has several nicknames, including Crescent City and the Big Easy. Though it is a major port city, it is considered to be much less frantic, much more slow-paced than any other major city, particularly in comparison to New York City. Located on the banks of the Mississippi River, the city, along with other areas in the Gulf region, were hit by Hurricane Katrina in 2005, leaving areas severely devastated, though the resiliency of its residents have inspired the country while the city is under reconstruction. The city's most famous strip, Bourbon Street in the French Quarter, continues to be known for its lively music, hosting duties for its annual Mardi Gras festivities in the winter, and its delicious Southern cuisine.

Left, Bald Cypress at sunset on Lake Martin. Louisiana, USA.

Maison Bourbon, on Bourbon Street, French Quarter, New Orleans. Louisiana, USA. Right, Bourbon street and the new town in the fog, French Quarter, New Orleans. Louisiana, USA.

The South

Beautiful North America 141

Wheelboats, Memphis. Tennessee, USA. Right, Bald cypress trees covered with Spanish moss, Lake Martin. Louisiana, USA.

The South

Chapter 8

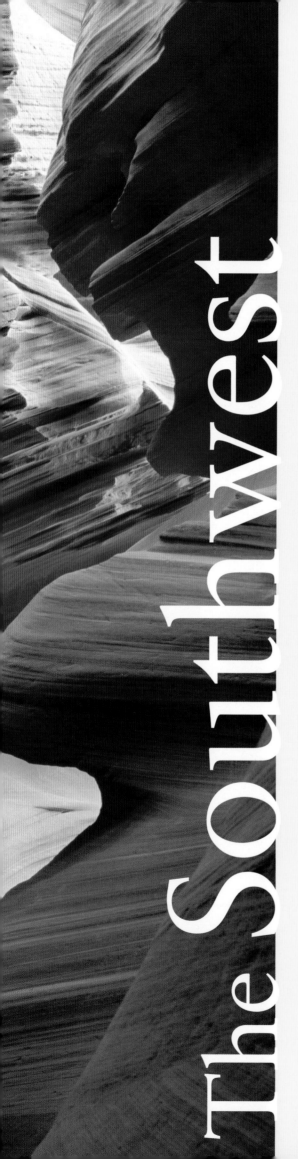

The Southwest

Right, Lower Antelope Canyon. Arizona, USA. Left, Cactus and Sonoyta Valley, dusk. Organ Pipe Cactus National Monument, Arizona, USA

From the multicolored mountains of Utah to the natural monuments of New Mexico, from the cactus-filled deserts of Arizona to the glitz, glamour, and lights of Las Vegas, the Southwest — or the American Southwest, as some call it — is diverse in its landscape, but also its people. The region is much more ethnically diverse than its neighboring states, both to the north and east of the area, with significant populations of Spanish Americans, American Indians, and Mexican Americans, which has contributed to its culture and history. The term "Tex-Mex," which means a merging of Texas and Mexican influences on mostly cuisine, was popularized in this area.

The heat, the dryness, the climate is something that some are familiar with when it comes to the Southwest. Temperatures can reach well over 100 degrees Fahrenheit during the dog days of summer, but even during winter and fall, certain states don't go below 80 degrees. The climate is the main contributor to its one-of-a-kind scenery, topography, geography, and animal life. Utah's famous Bryce Canyon National Park is, ironically, not a canyon at all but a natural amphitheatre. Located close to Zion National Park and the Grand Canyon, Bryce is much higher in elevation than either one of the two, reaching up to 9,000 feet. Sharp spires called hoodoos point up into the sky throughout this park, created by erosion. The highest point can reach up to 200 feet, while a series of the amphitheaters can cross over 20 miles. The largest amphitheater is Bryce Amphitheater, which is 12 miles long, 3 miles wide and 800 feet deep.

Utah also boasts Arches National Park, which contains over 2,000 natural sandstone arches. Near Moab, Utah, the park is over 100 square miles and reaches over 5,000 feet at its highest elevation. The past 30 years has seen over 40 arches

Hall of Giants, these formations are six stories tall. Carlsbad Caverns National Park, New Mexico, USA. Left, Thor's Hammer, mid-morning. Bryce Canyon National Park, Utah, USA.

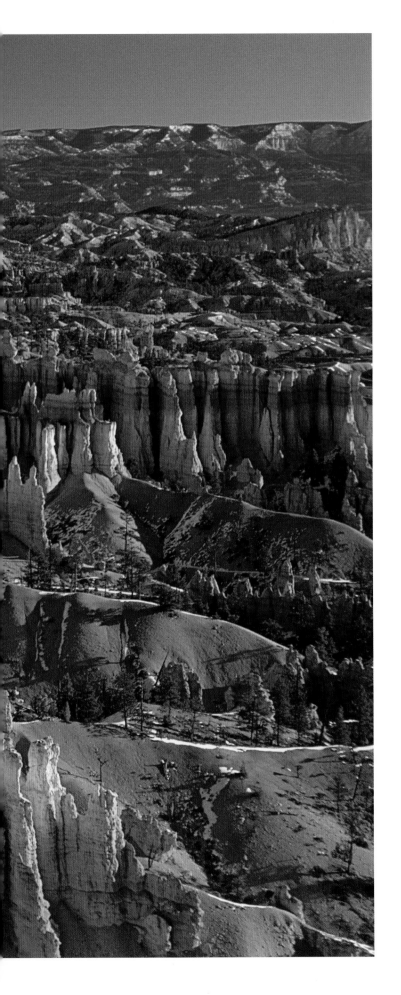

Fence, Old barn, horse and cliffs, Fruita. Capitol Reef National Park, Utah, USA. Left, Queen's Garden from Sunset Point, morning. Bryce Canyon National Park, Utah, USA.

Waterpocket fold from Strike Valley overlook, sunset. Capitol Reef National Park, Utah, USA. Below, Delicate Arch, winter sunset. Arches National Park, Utah, USA.

Above, Needles at sunset. Canyonlands
National Park, Utah, USA. Center, Snake Range
seen from the East above a pond. Great Basin
National Park, Nevada, USA.

Havasu Falls, Havasu Canyon. Grand Canyon National Park, Arizona, USA. Right, Ancient Bristlecone Pine, Wheeler Peak Basin, afternoon. Great Basin National Park, Nevada, USA.

Temples at Dawn from Yvapai Point. Grand Canyon National Park, Arizona, USA. Right, Colorado River and Cliffs at Toroweap, late afternoon. Grand Canyon National Park, Arizona, USA.

Above left, Tall cactus on the slopes of Tucson Mountains, late afternoon. Saguaro National Park, Arizona, USA. Above right, Saguaro cactus and moon at dawn. Saguaro National Park, Arizona, USA. Left, Colorful petrifieds logs in Blue Mesa, afternoon. Petrified Forest National Park, Arizona, USA.

From the multicolored mountains of Utah to the natural monuments of New Mexico, from the cactus-filled deserts of Arizona to the glitz, glamour, and lights of Las Vegas, the Southwest — or the American Southwest, as some call it — is diverse in its landscape, but also its people. The region is much more ethnically diverse than its neighboring states, both to the north and east of the area, with significant populations of Spanish Americans, American Indians, and Mexican Americans, which has contributed to its culture and history. The term "Tex-Mex," which means a merging of Texas and Mexican influences on mostly cuisine, was popularized in this area.

The heat, the dryness, the climate is something that some are familiar with when it comes to the Southwest. Temperatures can reach well over 100 degrees Fahrenheit during the dog days of summer, but even during winter and fall, certain states don't go below 80 degrees. The climate is the main contributor to its one-of-a-kind scenery, topography, geography, and animal life. Utah's famous Bryce Canyon National Park is, ironically, not a canyon at all but a natural amphitheatre. Located close to Zion National Park and the Grand Canyon, Bryce is much higher in elevation than either one of the two, reaching up to 9,000 feet. Sharp spires called hoodoos point up into the sky throughout this park, created by erosion. The highest point can reach up to 200 feet, while a series of the amphitheaters can cross over 20 miles. The largest amphitheater is Bryce Amphitheater, which is 12 miles long, 3 miles wide and 800 feet deep.

Superstition Mountains and brittlebush, Lost Dutchman State Park, dusk. Arizona, USA. Right, White House Anasazi ruins and wall with desert varnish. Canyon de Chelly National Monument, Arizona, USA.

Mittens and fog, sunrise. Monument Valley Tribal Park, Navajo Nation, Arizona and Utah, USA. Left, Ondulating rock formation, the Wave. Coyote Buttes, Vermilion cliffs National Monument, Arizona, USA

Yuccas and gypsum dunes, dawn, White Sands National Monument. New Mexico, USA. Right, Needles at sunset.
Canyonlands National Park, Utah, USA.

Buildings on main street and church, sunset, Austin. Nevada, USA.
Left, Playa with mud cracks, dawn. Black Rock Desert, Nevada, USA.

Elephant-shaped rock, Valley of Fire State Park. Nevada, USA. Right, Reeds and branches in marsh, sunrise, Havasu National Wildlife Refuge. Nevada, USA.

Generators in the power plant. Hoover Dam, Nevada and Arizona, USA. Right, The Strip at night seen from above. Las Vegas, Nevada, USA.

The Southwest

Beautiful North America   169

Right, Cliffs near Muley Point, sunset. Utah, USA. Above, Lone pine on sandstone swirl, Zion Plateau. Zion National Park, Utah, USA.

Right, Terraced cascades, Left Fork of the North Creek. Zion National Park, Utah, USA. Above, Water flowing in pools in the Subway, Left Fork of the North Creek. Zion National Park, Utah, USA.

Chapter 9

The Pacific States

Left, Lupines and Mt Rainier from Sunrise, morning. Mount Rainier National Park, Washington, USA. Far left, Live lava flow at dawn near the end of Chain of Craters road. Hawaii Volcanoes National Park, Hawaii, USA.

History has shown that settlers had dreams of "going west." Hearing about land, opportunities, and gold. The reality of the West was not that different than the fantasy. Sun, a vast expanse of land, and, in some areas, there were riches to be found. Though younger in its history, the West has somehow maintained its promise of a dream.

With coastlines on the Pacific Ocean, many of the early settlers came from New England. Portland, Oregon, for example, was named after Portland, Maine. Rain in the Northwest states create the lushness of forests and foliage, the mix of sun, rain, and desert climates create an environment described by many as "paradise," in places such as Southern California. And then there are the Hawaiian Islands, where beauty abounds from every inch of land, surf, and sun.

Some of the most famous landmarks can be found in this region of the country. The Golden Gate Bridge in San Francisco is just as famous as New York's Brooklyn Bridge; Yosemite National Park welcomes over three million visitors a year; California's city of Palm Springs is the state's desert paradise; and Hawaii's North Shore not only inspired a movie, but hails as one of the foremost spots to surf in the world.

Near Fresno, California, Sequoia National Park is one of the most visited parks in the country. The park was only the third national park to be formed in America, spanning over 400,000 acres. Though the park ranges from over 14,000 feet high in elevation to as low as 1,700, it is best known for its gargantuan Sequoia trees, including the General Sherman tree, the largest tree on Earth. Sitting in the Giant Forest, General Sherman is one of five (out of ten) of the largest trees on earth.

Trees with hoar frost above the Lake. Crater Lake National Park, Oregon, USA. Above right, Colorful cinder in Haleakala crater seen from White Hill. Haleakala National Park, Hawaii, USA. Below right, Tracks, moving rock on the Racetrack, late afternoon. Death Valley National Park, California, USA.

Over 2,000 miles from the mainland, the Hawaiian islands float on the Pacific Ocean. Recognized as one of the most beautiful spots in the world, Hawaii is the southernmost state in the country, consisting of eight islands: Kauai, Oahu, Maui, Hawaii, Niihau, Molokai, Lanai, and Kahoolawe. The islands continue to grow, though, as lava activity is still vigorous.

Above, Polynesian god statues in Puuhonua o Honauau (Place of Refuge). Big Island, Hawaii, USA. Below, Black sand beach at Punaluu. Big Island, Hawaii, USA. Left, Volcanic rocks and waves at sunrise, Keanae Peninsula. Maui, Hawaii, USA

Boulders, surf, and Na Pali Coast, Kee Beach, dusk. Kauai island, Hawaii, USA

Left, Palm trees and empty beach, Hanauma Bay. Oahu island, Hawaii, USA. Right, Waipoo falls and Waimea Canyon, afternoon. Kauai island, Hawaii, USA.

The Pacific States

Joshua trees, sunset. Joshua Tree National Park, California, USA.

Above, Painted dunes and pine trees. Lassen Volcanic National Park, California, USA. Center, Sequoias in Grant Grove, winter. Kings Canyon National Park, California, USA. Above right, Wildflowers and Mt Rainier from Paradise, late afternoon. Mount Rainier National Park, Washington, USA. Below right, Alabama hills and Mt Whitney, dawn. Sequoia National Park, California, USA.

The Pacific States

Above left, Mosses, trees, and pond, Quinault rain forest. Olympic National Park, Washington, USA. Above right, Tall redwood trees in fog, Lady Bird Johnson grove. Redwood National Park, California, USA. Right, Rododendrons, redwoods, and fog, Del Norte. Redwood National Park, California, USA.

Palm trees and fields in oasis, Coachella Valley. California, USA. Right, Grasses and Tufa towers, morning. Mono Lake, California, USA.

Above left, Victorians at Alamo Square and skyline, dusk. San Francisco, California, USA. Above right, Golden Gate bridge and fog seen from Battery Spencer, afternoon. San Francisco, California, USA. Left, Rocks and surf near Rocky Cny Bridge, Garapata State Park, dusk. Big Sur, California, USA.

The region claims the largest state in population and the third largest in terms of area: California. Currently, the population of this state alone is larger than that of 196 countries. California is a massive state, spanning over 150,000 miles and accommodating popular cities, such as San Francisco, San Diego, Santa Barbara, and Los Angeles. The latter, known as the City of Angels, is the largest city in the state, and the second-largest in the U.S. At its highest, L.A. reaches over 5,000 feet high, with its river, the Los Angeles River, crossing over almost all concrete.

Heading north, Washington State is not only known for its lush greenery, that grows everywhere, from the borders of the freeways to gardens, but it's also a vital metropolitan center. Olympic Peninsula is among the rainiest places in the world and the only rainforest in the continental United States. But the state also boasts deserts, high mountain ranges, and the deep blue Pacific Ocean that borders the state. Seattle, Washington, has become one of the most popular urban areas in the country.

One of the most beautiful and best-known national parks in the country, Yosemite, resides in the Pacific States. The park, which spans over 1,000 miles, contains five major vegetation sectors: lower montane; upper montane; subalpine; alpine; and chaparral and oak woodland. The park is truly a wonder, as it has over 160 rare plants (that are recorded) and has an elevation range of 2,000 to over 13,000.

Above, California Poppies, purple flowers, and hill.
Antelope Valley, California, USA. Grant Street at dusk,
Chinatown. San Francisco, California, USA. Right,
Sunset and clouds above Mt Shasta. California, USA.

The Pacific States

Walt Disney Concert Hall, early morning. Los Angeles, California, USA. Left, Lupine, Gorman Hills. California, USA.

Ferris Wheel and pier reflected on wet sand at night. Santa Monica, Los Angeles, California, USA.

Bridge, Harbor Freeway, and skyline at night. Los Angeles, California, USA.

Field with plowing lines, The Palouse. Washington, USA. Left, Seattle skyline at night with the Needle. Washington, USA.

Above left, Valley View in winter with fresh snow. Yosemite National Park, California, USA. Above right, Lighthouse at Haceta Head. Oregon, USA. Right, Lower Yosemite Falls, dusk. Yosemite National Park, California, USA.

Valley and Rainbow from Tunnel View, afternoon storm
light. Yosemite National Park, California, USA.

Chapter 10

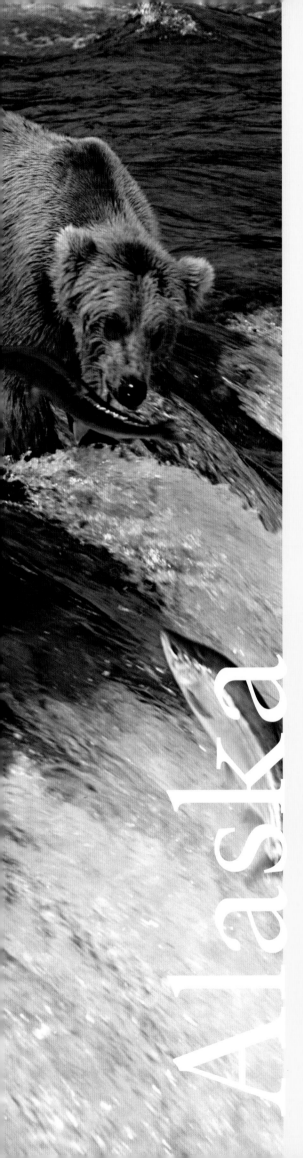

Alaska

Brown bear trying to catch leaping salmon at Brooks falls. Katmai National Park, Alaska, USA. Left, Translucent Iceberg near Mc Bride glacier, Muir inlet. Glacier Bay National Park, Alaska, USA.

In many ways, Alaska is the most original state in the U.S. First of all, it is the only noncontiguous state in the country; it is the only other state, along with Hawaii, that is not bordered by another state — with about 500 miles of Canadian land separating Alaska and Washington — making it the only mainland state that is reachable only by air and sea. And it is the largest state, by far. For all of these reasons, many citizens forget that it is part of the United States.

The state is so big, in fact, that it's easiest to identify it by regions. At over 500,000 square miles, Alaska is normally broken up into four distinct areas: South Central Alaska is along the coast and contains most of the state's population, including one of its most visited spots, Anchorage; Alaska Panhandle contains its capital, Juneau; Alaska Interior includes several rivers and the Arctic tundra; and the Alaska Bush is the most isolated area in the state.

One of the biggest draws of the area is the iceberg formations and glaciers. Every year, thousands of tourists flock onto cruise ships to catch a glimpse of these natural wonders. Because of the location of its glaciers, Juneau's Glacier Bay National Park is not accessible by land, only by ferry or airplane. The most famous of the formations has been named Muir Glacier, which spans over 200 feet tall and two miles wide.

More than any other state in the country, though, Alaska is known for its unfettered natural resources. With so much of its scenery inaccessible or, at the very least, challenging to reach, it has kept these natural marvels in their original form. One example of this is northwestern Alaska's Kobuk Valley National Park, which has no clear trails or roads. In contrast to the arctic weather and glaciers, the park contains the Kobuk Sand Dunes, as well as serves as the path for caribou migration — when visiting during the winter, tourists can witness caribou herds on their trek or, at the very least, see the animal's tracks all over the dunes. With over 1.7 million acres, the park is accessible only by foot, dogsled, snowmobile and by air, and is one of the least visited parks in the country. On the other end of the state, in south-central Alaska, the Kenai Fjords National Park includes the Harding Icefield, one of the largest in the United States. Kenai Fjords happens to be one of only three parks that is reachable by road. At its entrance, named Exit Glacier, a walk will take you right to the site of a massive glacier.

Its statistics in regard to its landscape is impressive — and are like no other region in the country. Alaska contains numerous islands, over three million lakes, over 16,000 square miles of its land is covered by glaciers, ice and wetlands cover over 180,000 square miles. Rich in culture, over 90 languages are spoken in Alaska, including 20 that are indigenous to the state. Tourists flock to Anchorage, Alaska, which is also the city that has its largest population, but its capital, Juneau, is not far behind.

Left, Alatna River valley near Circle Lake, evening. Gates of the Arctic National Park, Alaska, USA.

Long Lake with Autum Aspens, late afternoon. Glenn Highway, Central Alaska, USA. Right, Icebergs in Portage Lake with mountain reflexions. Alaska, USA.

Above left, Caribou tracks and ripples in the Great Sand Dunes. Kobuk Valley National Park, Alaska, USA. Above right, Lupine and mountains near Portage. Seward Highway, Kenai Peninsula, Alaska, USA.

Wildflowers and Exit Glacier, late afternoon. Kenai Fjords National Park, Alaska, USA.

Above, Tundra, braided rivers, Alaska Range in the evening from Polychrome Pass. Denali National Park, Alaska, USA. Below, Aerial view of meandering Alatna river and mountains. Gates of the Arctic National Park, Alaska, USA. Left, Tern Lake in late afternoon. Seward Highway, Kenai Peninsula, Alaska, USA

Margerie Glacier. Glacier Bay National Park, Alaska, USA.

Alaska

Icebergs near Mc Bride glacier, Muir inlet. Glacier Bay National Park, Alaska, USA.

216 Alaska

East end of Turquoise Lake. Lake Clark National Park, Alaska, USA. Center, Deep gorge carved by the Lethe River, Valley of Ten Thousand Smokes. Katmai National Park, Alaska, Above left, Aerial view of Harding icefield, fjords in the backgound. Kenai Fjords National Park, Alaska, USA. Below left, Mt Blackburn and Kennicott glacier seen from Mt Donoho, morning. Wrangell-St Elias National Park, Alaska, USA.

Mt Mc Kinley above Wonder Lake, evening. Denali National Park, Alaska, USA. Left, Twin Lakes, evening. Lake Clark National Park, Alaska, USA.

Chapter 11

Canada

Alberta, British Columbia, New Brunswick, Newfoundland and Labrador, Nova Scotia, Ontario, Prince Edward Island, Quebec, and Saskatchewan. The ten provinces that reside within its three territories — Northwest Territories, Nunavut, and Yukon Territory — together make up this country, yet individually are quite independent from the federal government.

From the Atlantic Ocean to the Pacific and northward touching the Arctic Ocean, Canada is the second-largest country, taking up most of North America. It borders America, and lies in between the U.S. and one of its states, Alaska.

Cities such as Ontario, Calgary, Toronto, Montreal, and Vancouver are a few of the most familiar metropolitan areas. The country is also known for mixing a little bit of country into its urban life. Nature abounds in Canada, no matter where you are. Metropolitan areas are acknowledged as cleaner, with an eye toward better upkeep than some of the most popular cities in the world. Southern Alberta holds Calgary, the largest city in that province. A destination for winter activities, the world became familiar with the city after it was chosen to host the Olympic Winter Games in 1988. Alberta can also claim to hold the country's first national park. Banff National Park was established in 1885 and spans over 2,000 miles. The majesty of Banff, though, lies in its variation. Mountains, glaciers, deep forests, and ice fields that dot its landscape have made this one of the most well-known and popular spots for tourists.

River, snow, and peak emerging from clouds. Banff National Park, Canadian Rockies, Alberta, Canada.

Skyline and tower, late afternoon. Calgary, Alberta, Canada.

Above, Cavell Lake and Mt Edith Cavell, sunrise. Jasper National Park, Canadian Rockies, Alberta, Canada. Below, Wenkchemna Peaks above Moraine Lake, mid-morning. Banff National Park, Canadian Rockies, Alberta, Canada. Left, Boulders, Lake Louise, and Victoria Peak, sunrise. Banff National Park, Canadian Rockies, Alberta, Canada

Beautiful North America

Prince of Wales hotel over Waterton Lakes, dusk. Waterton Lakes National Park, Alberta, Canada. Right, Spirit Island and Maligne Lake, afternoon. Jasper National Park, Canadian Rockies, Alberta, Canada. Left: Above, Red paintbrush flowers, daisies, and mountains. Banff National Park, Canadian Rockies, Alberta, Canada. Below, Badlands and hills, Dinosaur Provincial Park. Alberta, Canada. Maligne Lake, the largest in the Canadian Rockies, sunset. Jasper National Park, Canadian Rockies, Alberta, Canada.

Burrard Bridge, harbor, and high-rise residential buildings. Vancouver, British Columbia, Canada

Canada

Indian Teepees, Head-Smashed-In Buffalo Jump. Alberta, Canada.

British Columbia contains one of the most beautiful cities in the world, Vancouver. Though it is considered a major metropolitan area, the city is also recognized as one of the cleanest. Ironically, Vancouver is not located on the Vancouver Island, yet both are named after Captain George Vancouver of Great Britain, a navy captain who explored the country in the 18th century.

Far from Hollywood, Canada has become somewhat of its northern partner. With significant tax breaks made available to the industry, cities such as Toronto and Vancouver, whose scenery can mimic many different landscapes, have made it attractive for production, to the dismay of some American states. Toronto, the capital of Ontario, has a population of over two million people is the fifth most populous municipality in North America. Not only is it the most ethnically diverse in Canada, but is considered to be one of the most diverse cities in the world. Accommodating a major university, a vibrant cultural center, and a financial district, as well as its own film festival, the city is one of Canada's most important cities.

A little-known fact about Canada is that it contains the second-largest French-speaking city in the world, after Paris, France: Montreal. Though it is actually an island, with the St. Lawrence River wrapping around its west, south, and east sides, a smaller river borders around its northern end. Tourists flock to the city, where commercial property filled with shopping opportunities, world-renowned cuisine choices, and cultural institution surround cobblestone streets.

Left, Boats in inner harbour and parliament building lights. Victoria, British Columbia, Canada.

Cargo ship in harbor a sunrise. Vancouver, British Columbia, Canada. Rock and bay at sunset, Half-moon bay. Pacific Rim National Park, Vancouver Island, British Columbia, Canada.

Rainbow formed in the mist of Takakkaw Falls. Yoho National Park, Canadian Rockies, British Columbia, Canada. Center, Ocean and coastal range. Pacific Rim National Park, Vancouver Island, British Columbia, Canada.

Hostel at night, Quebec City. Quebec, Canada.
Below, Interior of Basilique Notre Dame,
Montreal. Quebec, Canada.

Lighted cabins and mountains reflected in Emerald Lake at night. Yoho National Park, Canadian Rockies, British Columbia, Canada

Mitchell range, Kootenay River, and flowers, sunset. Kootenay National Park, Canadian Rockies, British Columbia, Canada.

Canada

Daisies, fireweed, and Kootenay Valley, late afternoon. Kootenay National Park, Canadian Rockies, British Columbia, Canada. Right, Sunken Garden. Butchart Gardens, Victoria, British Columbia, Canada.

Chapter 12

Mexico

Right, Templo de Guadalupe and ocean, morning, Puerto Vallarta, Jalisco. Jalisco, Mexico. Left, Corridor in art gallery, Tlaquepaque. Jalisco, Mexico.

Bordered at the north by the United States and down south by Guatemala and Belize, Mexico's official name is Estados Unidos Mexicanos (the United Mexican States). One of the most colorful countries in the world, Mexico is also the most populated Spanish-speaking country in the world.

Cities such as Mexicali, Juarez, Tijuana, Guadalajara, and Mexico City are a few urban areas with the largest populations. Destinations such as Acapulco, Puerto Vallerta, and Cabo San Lucas are better known for their beaches and, subsequent, resorts, which attract tourists from everywhere. For this reason, Mexico has become a particularly popular spring break spot for students. Apart from the reputation that some of these places have received — of strictly being a resort destination — the beauty of Mexico's landscape is impossible to miss. Puerto Vallarta, which resides in the state of Jalisco, was a traditional village founded in 1851. After becoming a municipality, Hollywood came calling, and director John Huston decided to use it as the backdrop for his film "The Night of the Iguana."

Mexico's history is still evident in its architecture and scenery. Though the country itself is modernizing at a quick pace, its roots run deep. Guanajuato is an example of this very aspect of the country. Located at the center of Mexico, about three hours away from Mexico City, Guanajuato translates into the phrase "hill of frogs." The city still produces tin, gold, copper, and lead, among other things, extracted from its silver mines — some of the best in the world. Along with its history, it is also one of the most productive cities, manufacturing everything from shoes to auto parts to harvesting fruits and vegetables.

Elderly man walking along a colorful wall, Tlaquepaque. Jalisco, Mexico.

Stairway ceiling with portrait of angry Miguel Hidalgo by Jose Clemente Orozco. Guadalajara, Jalisco, Mexico.

Above, Cactus amongst blue agaves. Mexico. Right, Field of agaves near Tequila. Mexico.

Above, Street crossing and Cathedral, late afternoon.
Guadalajara, Jalisco, Mexico. Center, Footbridge above Rio
Cuale at dusk, Puerto Vallarta, Jalisco. Jalisco, Mexico.

Above right, Glass spheres, Tonala. Jalisco, Mexico. Below right, Tequila distillery, Puerto Vallarta, Jalisco. Jalisco, Mexico.

Palm-tree fringed swimming pool at sunset, Nuevo Vallarta, Nayarit. Jalisco, Mexico.

Rural scene with banana trees, palm tree, horses, and field. Mexico.

Jalisco's capital city, Guadalajara, is also the country's second most populated, one notch below Mexico City. Credited as the birthplace of mariachi music, some consider Guadalajara to be the most "Mexican," as so many of Mexico's cultural influences have derived from the area. One of the most popular soccer teams, Chivas Rayadas, come from the city, while its landscape is the most beautiful in the country.

Though the country is very much a part of North America, it is the most populated Latin American nation in the world. As for its total territory, Mexico also includes islands, such as the Guadalupe and the Revillagigedo Islands. The Rio Grande borders the city of Juarez east of the Gulf of Mexico, while there are more abstract symbols that delineate the land borders between the United States and Mexico. Its coastline is one of the most spectacular in the world, known for its warm, crystal-blue water and white sand. It butts up against several bodies of water, including the Pacific Ocean, the Gulf of California, the Gulf of Mexico, and the Caribbean Sea.

The culture of the country has become one of the most influential in the world, especially in the past century. Its music, art, cuisine, literature all have pervaded through countries all over the world. Mexican folk art is known for its colorful embroidery that covers everything from rugs, baskets, and clothing.

But, arguably, it's the country's cuisine that has made the most impact. One of the richest, most distinct foods in the world, Mexican cuisine can be found almost everywhere today. Dishes such as enchiladas, tacos, tamales are all well-known, everyday foods.

Left, Avenue Hidalgo with Teatro Calderon at night. Zacatecas, Mexico.

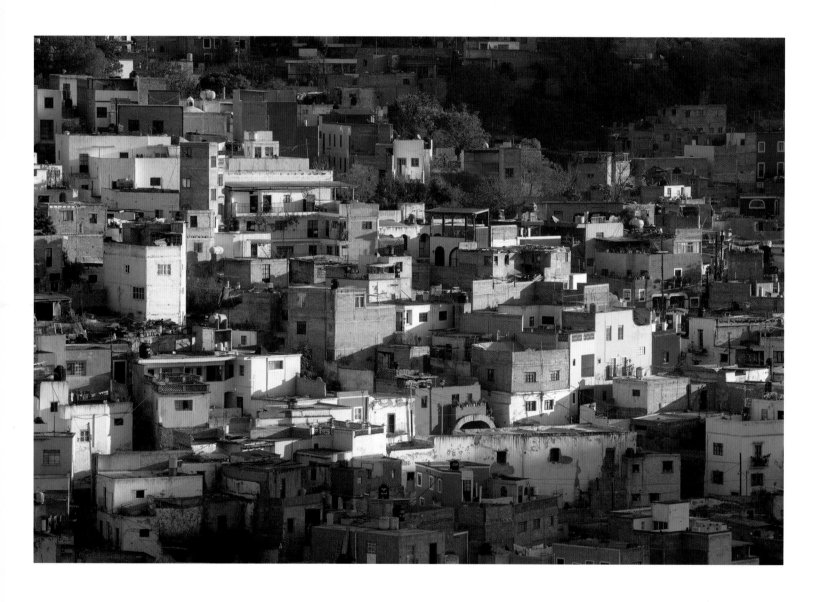

Vividly colored houses on hill, early morning. Guanajuato, Mexico. Right, Houses and Cajaon de Garcia Rojas. Zacatecas, Mexico.

Mexico

LAS CALLAS

el Raspanieve
Sucursal de los Únicos y Originales Raspanieves de Jerez

Hidalgo avenue and Cathdedral, morning. Zacatecas, Mexico.

Above left, Panoramic view of the historic town with illuminated basilic, university, and La Compania. Guanajuato, Mexico. Above right, Man walking down stairs of Cajaon de Garcia Rojas. Zacatecas, Mexico.

Cerro de la Bufa and town at night. Zacatecas, Mexico. Left, Cathedral and town, late afternoon. Zacatecas, Mexico.